OUR WILDLIFE WORLD

PENGUINS

Merebeth Switzer

Grolier

FACTS IN BRIEF

Classification of the penguins

    Class: *Aves* (birds)

    Order: *Sphenisciformes* (penguins)

    Family: *Spheniscidae* (penguin family)

    Genus: There are six genera of penguins.

    Species: There are eighteen species of penguins.

World distribution.   Penguins are found only in the seas of the Southern Hemisphere.

Habitat.   Ocean and rocky coasts.

Distinctive physical characteristics.   Penguins are flightless birds adapted for life in the ocean with webbed feet and small flipper-like wings.

Habits.   Lay and hatch eggs in large groups; males and females share in the raising of the young.

Diet.   Fish, crustaceans and small squids.

This series is approved and recommended by the Federation of Ontario Naturalists.

Canadian Cataloguing in Publication Data

Switzer, Merebeth
  Penguins

(Nature's children)
Issued also in French under title: Les manchots.
Includes index.
ISBN 0-7172-2482-1

1. Penguins—Juvenile literature.   I. Title.   II. Series.

QL696.S473S93 1988   j598.4'41   C88-094664-4

Contents

Two black and white shapes zip through the water, plunging and diving at incredible speeds. At first, they appear to be fish. But look closer and you will see that they are penguins.

Penguins are amazingly agile. Sometimes they swim towards each other so quicky you expect them to crash. Then, at the last moment, *swoosh!* Without any warning they somersault, turn and streak away. These black and white daredevil birds are perfectly at home "flying" through the ocean. Turn the page to find out more about these underwater acrobats.

Penguins do not fly through the air, but they do through water!

Home Sweet Home

When someone says the word *penguin* do you think of snowstorms and polar bears? If you do, you will be surprised to learn that these images are only partly true.

Penguins are only found in the southern hemisphere, that is the part of the world that lies south of the equator. Polars bears live in the Arctic, which is the northernmost part of the world. This means that penguins and polar bears are never seen together in the wild.

The idea of a penguin being at home in the ice and snow is correct . . . at least for some species. But there are 18 different types of penguins, and some are found on the coasts of Australia, New Zealand, South Africa, Chile and Peru, and even on the Galapagos Islands at the equator!

The shaded area on this map shows where penguins live.

SOUTH AMERICA

AFRICA

South Pole

ANTARCTICA

NEW ZEALAND

AUSTRALIA

Big Penguins, Little Penguins

When dinosaurs roamed the earth, the penguin's giant ancestor towered 1.5 metres (5 feet) tall. Now penguins are smaller. The largest is the Emperor Penguin, which may be the same height and weight as a ten-year-old. The smallest penguin is the Little or Fairy Penguin of Australia, which is only 35 centimetres (14 inches) tall and weighs 1 kilogram (2.2 pounds).

The smaller penguins are found closer to the equator. The biggest penguins—the Emperor, King, Adelie, Gentoo and Chinstrap—are found in the Antarctic. Their larger bodies keep warmer longer than the bodies of their smaller cousins. And keeping warm is important in the Antarctic!

Black and White

Did you ever wonder why penguins are black and white? As with many animals, the penguin's color pattern acts as camouflage and helps protect it from predators. Here's how it works. The dark back blends in with the dark waters of the ocean when viewed from above, making the penguin hard to spot by a predator looking down. On the other hand, if a hungry Killer Whale or Leopard Seal approaches from underneath, the white belly makes the penguin almost invisible against the sunny surface of the sea.

Of course, this black and white pattern is of little help on land, but adult penguins have few predators there. Killer Whales cannot follow them ashore, and seals and sea lions aren't fast enough to catch a penguin on land.

The Black-footed Penguin has an ideal coat for camouflage.

Penguin Patterns

We all know that penguins are black and white, but did you know that each species has a specific black and white color pattern?

Some penguins have black lines on their chests or necks while others have white spots on their heads. So it's easy to tell one type from another.

Moreover, most species of penguins aren't *just* black and white. Some have red or pink beaks while others have orange or red feet. A few have bright red or yellow eyes and some have patches of orange or yellow on their heads or chests. And there are even a few species that have tufts of bright feathers around their eyes that look like bushy eyebrows.

The Macaroni Penguin is unusual because of the long colorful feathers on its head.

Penguins on Parade

One of the penguin's most endearing features is its upright waddle across the ice with its wings spread out at its side. A penguin is not built quite like other birds, whose legs are near the center of their bodies. Instead, a penguin's legs are far back on its body near the tail. This causes it to walk upright, just like people.

The penguin uses its wings to balance on land but cannot lift them very high or fold them like other birds. This is because of the way the wing joint is built to help make swimming easier.

Waddling off into the sunset.

Diving Daredevils

Penguins spend more than two-thirds of their life swimming in the ocean. Their streamlined bodies, shaped like a submarine, move easily through the water, and they are expert swimmers. Pumping their stiff, flipper-like wings, they "fly" through the water, using their stubby tail and webbed feet as a rudder to steer.

Penguins are one of the top divers of animals that breathe air. Like the other champion divers, seals and whales, penguins are able to dive much deeper than humans. However, because penguins breathe air they cannot stay underwater too long.

Penguins can dive so well because they have solid bones. These bones give the birds added weight, which helps them to dive deep and to withstand the great pressure found underwater. Most other birds have hollow, lightweight bones, which are perfect for flying.

In some parts of the Antarctic Ocean penguins swim in water so cold that we would die if we took even a short dip.

Raincoats and Thermal Underwear

Penguins are birds and, like all birds, they have feathers. So how can they spend so much time frolicking in the ocean?

Penguin feathers are unique. They are very small, no longer than the bristles on your toothbrush. The tips are very stiff and they overlap like shingles to form a tight waterproof coat. This, and the natural oils from the penguin's skin, keep it dry.

Underneath the waterproof feathers is a thick coat of soft down right next to the bird's skin. This layer traps warm air near the penguin's body and keeps it snug against the cold winds and ocean waters. Some penguins even have a layer of fat, or blubber, under their skin for extra insulation. As well, tough pads on the bottom of the penguin's feet keep out the cold and stop them from freezing.

A pair of warmly dressed King Penguins.

A New Wardrobe

Each year, a penguin's feathers wear out and they must be replaced. New feathers under the skin begin to push through the old feathers. The old feathers fall out once the new ones have come in. This is called molting.

Molting takes a great deal of energy. During this time, which can last up to five weeks, a penguin may lose up to half its body weight! While molting the penguin must stay on land—because without its thick, protective coat to keep it warm and dry, it could not survive in the icy water.

Like all penguins King Penguins molt once a year.

A Seafood Feast

Even when penguins live as far north as the equator they will not swim in warm water. In fact, they will only enter the cold currents of the Antarctic Ocean, which flow throughout the southern hemisphere. These icy waters are particularly rich in the foods that penguins like best.

Penguins get all their food from the ocean but not all penguins eat the same things. The Macaroni Penguin—which got its name from the feathers behind its eyes which look like macaroni—feeds on squid and shrimp. The Peruvian Penguin prefers small fish, such as anchovies. While most penguins eat fish and shellfish, others also enjoy a large quantity of tiny, shrimp-like creatures called krill.

Penguins are big eaters. It is believed that they may eat more than half the food taken by predators in the southern oceans.

Adelie Penguins diving for a shrimp dinner.

Perfect Gentlemen?

Penguins may look like cute stuffed toys and perfect gentlemen in their "tuxedos," but that soft, cuddly image is very misleading. Penguins are hunters and they are built to survive. They have razor-sharp beaks which are perfect for catching and eating their dinner swiftly and efficiently. Their small wings may not look like much, but they are capable of delivering a mightly blow if an intruder should get too close to their nest.

The beak of the Black-footed Penguin is strong and sharp.

Cooling Off

It may seem strange that penguins need to cool off. But, as you know, some penguins are found in warm climates, and on sunny summer days in the Antarctic the temperature rises above freezing. That might not seem hot to you, but for the Emperor Penguin it is mighty warm.

One of the easiest ways a penguin can cool off is probably a trick you have tried yourself: a quick dip into water.

Another thing adult penguins can do is fluff up their feathers and let as much air as possible circulate close to their skin. When they do this, you can see their bright pink skin.

Sometimes a penguin will hold its wings away from the sides of its body or flap them. These actions let more air come in contact with blood vessels on the underside of the wing. And that also helps to cool down the penguin.

"I think I'm a little overdressed for this weather!" (Emperor Penguin)

Bobsledding Home

Each year, after many months of hunting and feeding at sea, penguins return to their nesting grounds. For some, this may involve a simple hop onto the shore or a short walk to a nearby cave. But for others it is a long trek.

Emperor and Adelie penguins nest inland more than 100 kilometres (60 miles) from the Antarctic ice shelf. If you have ever seen a penguin waddling along, you might wonder how they manage to make this long trip.

Actually, in soft snow, a penguin can run as fast as a person. But to cover long distances and to conserve energy, penguins turn themselves into little self-propelled toboggans. By flopping onto their tummies and using their wings and feet for propulsion, they can cover great distances quite quickly. In spite of the cold ice next to their bodies, the penguins are kept warm by all the exercise. Sometimes they may even have to stop and fluff out their feathers to cool off!

Opposite page:
Some penguins must travel long distances by land or by sea to reach their nesting grounds. They use the sun to navigate.

Love Birds

Although it is difficult for us to tell a male penguin from a female, or to recognize a particular penguin in a huge rookery full of them, penguins have no such problem. They can tell each other apart, and year after year they return to the rookeries to find their previous mates. Often male penguins arrive at the rookery first and start squabbling over the best nesting sites. Once they have staked out their territory, they patiently wait for their mates to arrive.

When the happy pair is reunited there is quite a display. Greetings may include braying, croaking, trumpeting and cooing. They beat their flippers, clack their bills and dance. As you can imagine this is a very noisy, chaotic time in the rookery.

Foot Nests

Most penguins lay two eggs. But the female King and Emperor penguins lay only one egg and they do so in the middle of the Antarctic winter. Once the egg is laid, the father penguin takes over. Using his beak, he nudges the egg on top of his feet and wriggles until it lies safely tucked away under a special flap of belly skin. For the next two months, he is left to care for the egg. The father penguins huddle together against the bitterly cold winter, moving little and eating nothing.

During this time, the females return to the ocean to feed and store up fat before they return to care for their young chick.

Fancy footwork! (King Penguin)

Building a Nest

Although the King and Emperor penguins have their own built-in nests, other penguins must build a nest for their eggs. These penguins often nest in open areas where there are not a lot of materials to use, so they have to make do with whatever is handy.

Many penguins, including those that nest on the rocky coast of Antarctica, collect small pebbles. A pebble nest helps to keep the eggs off the cold ground and prevents them from getting wet if the snow melts quickly or there is a sudden rainstorm.

Other penguins use coarse grass, twigs, moss and even seaweed for their nests. Sometimes these penguins build their nests inside rock crevices or burrows. At other times they may dig into the sand or down into the excrement, or guano, that has been left by thousands of generations of penguins. These hollows act as extra shelter against bad weather and predators.

An Adelie Penguin returns to the nest to offer its mate a pebble.

Hatching

Penguin chicks may take up to three days to break out of their shell completely. When they finally pop through, they are moist from the egg sack. They dry quickly into fluffy, downy balls, usually brown in color.

Emperor Penguin chicks are the only ones born without a covering of down feathers. They are kept warm by their father. How? He has a naked patch under his belly flap where he has plucked off all the feathers. This little ''hot spot'' is called a brood patch and it allows more of the parent's body heat to reach the egg. Then when the chick is born, its naked body helps it to get the most heat from the parent's body while it stays snuggled under the built-in shelter.

Penguin chicks rely on their parents not only for food but also for warmth. They cannot control their own body temperature for 2 weeks.

Penguin Parents

Both penguin parents share the task of caring for their young. Since eggs and baby penguins are very vulnerable they must be protected. Also, penguin chicks need so much food in their first weeks of life that the job is simply too big for one parent.

Penguin parents split the duties. One stands guard while the other goes off to bring back food for the hungry chick or chicks. Some penguins take regular turns at the two tasks, while others simply divide them, based on the parent's sex. Before Royal and Rockhopper chicks are born, for instance, the female sits on the nest while the male goes off to feed and store up fat for his stint of chick sitting. After the chicks are born, the father stands guard while the hen goes off to get food.

When mother returns she is carrying almost half her body weight in partially digested food. The chicks place their beaks inside mom's mouth. She then brings the food back up into her mouth for them to eat.

Opposite page: *Keeping this Gentoo Penguin chick fed is a full time job.*

Getting Bigger

Finally, the day comes when the chicks need more food than one parent can provide. The young are now left unguarded while both parents go off to collect food. For some male penguins it is finally a chance to start eating again. While collecting food for junior, of course. By this time the young have grown bigger and although they are not totally safe from hungry birds, such as skuas and sheathbills, they are capable of defending themselves.

This Black-footed Penguin chick will become black and white once its adult feathers grow in.

Penguin Daycare

Many kinds of penguins gather their young together into special nurseries, called crèches. Chicks move into the crèches as soon as they begin to walk, which may be anywhere from 10 to 45 days after they hatch.

Crèches are good for several reasons. Both parents can now find food knowing that their chick is not alone and, in cold climates, the chicks can huddle together for warmth. Also, the young are safer in a large group, because it is harder for hungry seabirds to choose a tasty morsel for dinner.

When a parent returns, it utters a few loud "Supper!" calls and the chick comes running. If another chick should happen by, it is ignored or even driven away by the parent.

A King and Gentoo crèche.

Swimming Lessons

Not all types of penguin chicks grow at the same rate. It takes Little Blue and Adelie penguins only two months to grow up while King Penguins take twelve to fourteen months. During this time their downy feathers are replaced by adult feathers. Penguin chicks cannot take to the water until they have this protective coat covering their body.

And then one day it happens. The penguin parents return to the rookery to feed their chick, only to find it is gone. The young one has decided it is time to head to the water to begin its ocean life. Without any lessons, the youngster plunges into the ocean and begins to swim.

To a penguin parent, the empty nest is a sign that their harried hunt to feed their chick is over. They too can return to the ocean.

Words to Know

Brood patch   A featherless patch on the underside of a penguin's body that allows body heat to warm incubating eggs and newly hatched chicks.

Camouflage   Colors and patterns that help an animal blend in with its surroundings.

Cock   A male penguin.

Colony   Large group of nesting birds.

Crèche   Nursery group into which penguin chicks may be gathered for warmth and safety while the parents hunt for food.

Guano   A bird's bodily wastes.

Hen   A female penguin.

Krill   Very small shrimp-like creatures that live in the ocean.

Mate   To come together to produce young. Either member of an animal pair is also the other's mate.

Molting   To shed one set of feathers and grow another.

Navigate   To find the way from one place to another.

Predator   An animal that hunts other animals for food.

Rookery   A colony.

INDEX

Cover Photo: Kjell B. Sandved
Photo Credits: Kjell B. Sandved, pages 4, 8, 19, 20, 23, 27, 31, 35, 40; Y.J. Rey-Millett, World Wildlife Fund, page 7; Bill Ivy, pages 11, 24, 43; Ian Strange, World Wildlife Fund, page 12; L.G. Ziesler, Hot Shots, page 15; Masterfile, page 16; Paul Drummond, Canapress, pages 28, 36; D. Roby, Academy of Natural Sciences, page 37; Dr. A. Sutter, World Wildlife Fund, page 44.